Italian Americans

CAROLYN P. YODER

Heinemann Library
Chicago, Illinois

© 2003 Heinemann Library
a division of Reed Elsevier Inc.
Chicago, Illinois

Customer Service 888-454-2279

Visit our website at www.heinemannlibrary.com

Created by the publishing team at Heinemann Library
Designed by Roslyn Broder
Photo research by Scott Braut
Printed and Bound in China by CTPS

10 09
10 9 8 7 6 5 4 3
ISBN 13 : 978 1403404213 (PB)

Library of Congress Cataloging-in-Publication Data
Yoder, Carolyn, 1953-
  Italian Americans / Carolyn Yoder.
      p. cm. -- (We are America)
Summary: An overview of the history and daily lives of Italian people who immigrated to the United States.
Includes bibliographical references (p.) and index.
  ISBN 1-40340-166-7 (lib. bdg.) -- ISBN 1-40340-421-6 (pbk.)
  1. Italian Americans--History--Juvenile literature. 2. Italian Americans--Social life and customs--Juvenile literature. [1. Italian Americans.] I. Title. II. Series.
  E184.I8 Y63 2002
  973'.0451--dc21

                                2002004141

Acknowledgments
The author and publishers are grateful to the following for permission to reproduce copyright material: pp. 4, 5, 28, 29 Courtesy of Louis Longo family; pp. 7, 9, 10, 12 Bettmann/Corbis; p. 8 B.W. Kilburn/Corbis; pp. 11, 23 UPI/Bettmann/Corbis; pp. 13, 14, 24 Hulton Archive; p. 16 Michael Maslan Historic Photographs/Corbis; p. 17 Lewis W. Hine Collection/National Archives and Records Administration; p. 18 Historical Society of Western Pennsylvania; pp. 19, 20, 21 Courtesy of Scott Braut; p. 22 P. L. Sperr/Archive Photos/Hulton Archive; p. 25 Courtesy of Jack Florence, Sr.; p. 26 Eduardo Migliaccio Papers, Box 1/ Immigration History Research Center/University of Minnesota; p. 27 New York Times Co./Archive Photos/Hulton Archive

Cover photographs provided by Bettman/Corbis (bck) and Scott Braut

Special thanks to Barry Moreno of the Ellis Island Immigration Museum for his comments in preparation of this book.

Some quotations and material used in this book come from the following sources. In some cases, quotes have been abridged for clarity: pp. 9, 11, 13 Courtesy of the Ellis Island Oral History Project of the Ellis Island Immigration Museum; p. 19 *In the Shadow of Liberty: The Chronicle of Ellis Island* by Edward Corsi (Manchester, N.H.: Ayer Company Publishers, 1969).

Some words are shown in bold, **like this.** You can find out what they mean by looking in the glossary.

For more information on the people on the cover of this book, turn to page 20. For more information on the image that appears in the background of the cover, turn to page 9.

Contents

One Teenager's Story

In 1905, thousands of people left southern Italy to come to the United States. Many of them were young men who wanted to be on their own and find jobs. Louis Longo was one of them. He was eighteen years old and living in a town called Benevento in southern Italy when he decided to leave Italy. Louis was studying to be a **priest,** but he was not happy. Louis traveled to Naples, Italy. There, he got on a **steamship** headed for New York City.

Louis left the U.S. to visit Italy in 1927. Seen above is his passport, a document he needed to travel there.

Like many other **immigrants,** Louis didn't know anyone in New York City. He moved to an area in the city where other Italians lived. He found a job making watches in a **jewelry** store. Louis met the woman he would one day marry, Theresa, at the store. She was also from southern Italy and had come to the United States when she was three.

This photo of Louis, Theresa, and their two children was taken in New York City.

My grandfather was proud to be an American. He felt that anyone could make it in the United States if they worked really hard.
—Jacqueline Greco, Louis Longo's granddaughter

Italy

Italy is a country in Europe. It is made up of a **peninsula,** which looks a lot like a boot, and two islands, Sardinia and Sicily. Most of Italy is surrounded by water. The northern part of Italy borders France, Switzerland, Austria, and Slovenia. Italy has two other countries inside of its borders, which are Vatican City and San Marino.

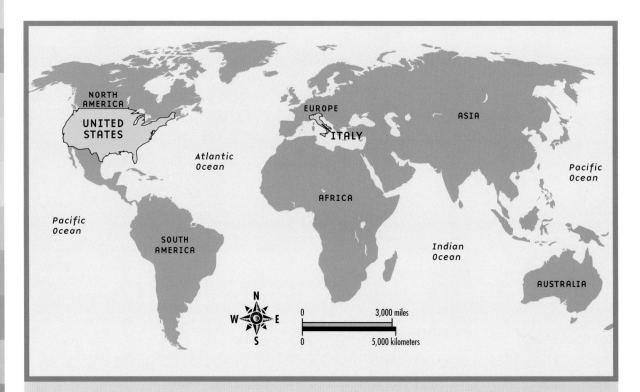

Italy became a republic, a country in which people vote to elect their leaders, in 1946. On this map, you can see where Italy and the United States are located.

This farming family is shown in 1919 in front of their home in southern Italy. They worked and lived on the island of Sicily.

In 1870, Italy became a unified independent country with a king as its leader. The next year, Rome became Italy's capital. At this time, the northern and southern parts of Italy were very different. Northern Italy had more businesses and cities. People in southern Italy lived in small villages and were mostly poor farmers. They also had a hard time living under the new government.

Southern Italy is called *Mezzogiorno*. This means "land of the midday sun."

Coming to America

*The Italians in the photo above had to leave Italy because their houses were destroyed by an **earthquake.***

From 1880 to 1921, millions of Italians came to live in the United States. Many of them planned to earn money and return to Italy. Most of them were from southern Italy. They worked as farmers on land they did not own. Many could not read or write. They had very little money.

People left Italy because there were too many people living there. They had to pay high taxes and rent. The land was also hard to farm. Diseases like **cholera** and **malaria** killed thousands of people. **Relatives** and friends in the United States also said they would be better off living in the United States.

Time Line

1820–1880	About 80,000 Italians come to the United States. Most of them are from northern Italy.
1880–1921	Millions of Italians come to the U.S. Most of them are from southern Italy.
1900	Half a million Italians live in the U.S.
1915–1919	Few leave Italy due to World War One.
1922–1943	Benito Mussolini rules Italy. Only a few Italians leave Italy.
1924	U.S. government passes a law that limits the number of **immigrants** allowed yearly.
1942	Only 69 Italians move to the U.S.
2000	About 2,700 Italians move to the U.S.

In 1900, Mulberry Street in New York City was home to many Italians.

I missed my father . . . So I . . . did nothing but sort of dream about being in America . . .
—Virgil C. Crisafulli, who came to the United States in 1922 from Sicily at the age of ten

The Voyage

Italian people took **steamships** to get to the United States. They left Italy from **port** cities like Naples, Genoa, and Palermo. The trip took about two weeks. The **immigrants** usually had to travel in **steerage** where it was crowded and dark. They could spend time on the **deck** unless there was stormy weather. The immigrants had never been on a big ship before and had no idea what the U.S. would be like.

This ship carried more than 2,000 passengers from Italy to New York City in 1920.

People did have some fun on the ships. They met people from other countries, played music, sang songs, and danced. These two immigrant girls are seeing New York **harbor** for the first time.

I never met so many people, and I never heard so many languages spoken.
—Elisa Boschi Salvi, talking about her 1915 trip to the United States. She was ten years old.

Arriving in America

Most of the **steamships** from Italy arrived in New York **harbor.** The passengers in **steerage** took long, flat boats to the Ellis Island **Immigration** Station. There, doctors looked at them to see if they had any diseases or **disabilities.** They were also asked questions like "Do you have any money?" or "What will you do for work?" People had to have some money to be allowed to enter the United States, but they could not already have jobs there.

Ellis Island opened in 1892. Immigrants, like this Italian family in 1905, had to wear tags on their clothes to show which ships they had been on.

This picture shows immigrants waiting to be looked at by doctors in 1904. Thousands of people went through Ellis Island each day.

People who had medical problems had to stay at the station to get better. Some had to wait for people to meet them. A few who were really sick had to return to Italy, but most of the people passed **inspection.** They met family members and friends and took **ferries** to New York or New Jersey. Some people then traveled by trains to other parts of the United States.

You just waited, I don't know if it was a day, or two days, or what . . . since my father lived in Ohio, he couldn't come to meet us. He gave us directions. We were to take a train from Ellis Island to Akron [Ohio].
— Virgil C. Crisafulli

Living in the United States

Many of the **immigrants** stayed in New York City. They moved to areas where other Italian Americans lived. Many joined family and friends. Life in New York City was hard. Most people lived in crowded **tenement houses.** Families often lived together in one small room. People spent time outside to get fresh air and to meet with friends. Children played games on city streets.

New York City's Little Italy looked like this in 1890.

These are some of the areas in the United States where Italians first came to and where many still live today.

Work was easier to find in big cities in the United States. About 340,000 Italian Americans lived in New York City by 1910. Others lived in Boston, Philadelphia, and Chicago. Societies were started to help Italian immigrants. They offered shelter and food and helped people find jobs and places to live. They also taught Italians how to speak English.

Frances Xavier Cabrini came to New York City from Italy in 1889. In Italy, she and a group of nuns had taken care of poor children. In the United States, she helped set up hospitals, schools, and **orphanages.** She became a U.S. citizen in 1909. She was the first U.S. citizen to become a **saint.**

Jobs

Most Italians who came to the United States did not work on farms like they had in Italy. They lived in cities and found jobs building streets, subways, bridges, tunnels, sewers, **skyscrapers,** and railroads. Women, men, and children also worked long hours in factories. Children often left school early to go to work. They earned money to help their families.

In about 1900, these Italian immigrants worked on railroads in New York.

This picture from 1910 shows Italian girls carrying baskets of fruit on their heads. They were picking berries in Delaware.

Italians who lived in western and southern states found jobs in mines and in lumber and steel mills. Some **immigrants** had special skills. They worked as bricklayers or carpenters and helped to build houses. Some Italian Americans were farmers and fishermen. Many used to do the same kind of work in Italy. The farmers lived all over the United States and grew vegetables, wheat, cotton, grapes, and other fruits.

In 1906, Generoso Pope came to the United States from Italy. He was fifteen. Pope grew up to own a New York newspaper written in Italian. It had the most readers of any Italian newspaper in the United States.

Living in the City

Many Italian Americans lived in city neighborhoods. They lived close to family members and friends who came from the same villages or areas in Italy. These neighborhoods became known as Little Italys. New York City's Little Italys were located in the Mulberry Bend, Greenwich Village, East Harlem, and Brooklyn neighborhoods. Philadelphia, Boston, and Chicago also had well-known Little Italys.

This 1950 photo shows a group of Italian Americans who owned and worked at Marasco's Grocery in Pittsburgh, Pennsylvania.

Domenico Paone, seen in the background, had a shoe shop in Jersey City, New Jersey. He arrived in New York from Italy in 1912.

Italian people could get anything they needed in Little Italy. Italian barbers, **tailors,** and shoemakers had businesses. There were bookstores, banks, and places to eat. There were theaters, music halls, and churches. People enjoyed living near people like them. They could share stories, play games, and celebrate important events and holidays together.

I began to feel dazed and lost, but it gave me a new grip on myself to arrive in Harlem's Little Italy and see and hear all about [my] people of my own nationality.

—Edward Corsi, who came to the United States in 1907 when he was ten years old

Families

In the late 1800s, most of the Italians that came to the United States were young men. Some planned to find work, earn money, and bring their families in Italy to the United States. Wives and children later joined their husbands and fathers. Families wanted to be together and not live in two different countries.

This family came to the state of New Jersey from an area in southern Italy called Calabria.

Vincenzo Vista and Eleanora La Grasta, seen on the left, were both from Molfetta, Italy. They were married on October 9, 1921, in the U.S.

Friends were also important in family life. **Godparents** helped raise children and watched over them. Births, baptisms, weddings, and funerals were important family events. At weddings, music played and people danced. The tarantella was a popular **folk** dance. Candy-covered almonds and *wanda,* fried dough covered with powdered sugar, were served to bring good luck.

At school, Italian children learned to speak English. Sometimes, their parents didn't learn English because most people they worked with and talked to were also Italian.

Customs and Celebrations

Most Italian Americans were **Roman Catholic.** They held festivals to honor their village **saints** or the **Virgin Mary.** The feast of Saint Joseph was held on March 19. Saint Joseph took care of families, the poor, and **orphans.** Italian Americans made **altars** on tables and asked Joseph to help them. Vegetable, pasta, and fish dishes and breads and sweets were placed on the altars. Families invited **relatives,** friends, and even strangers to eat these special foods.

In 1925, these Italian girls, shown in Little Italy in New York City, made an altar out of boxes that eggs came in.

These Italian Americans gathered to watch a parade in New York City on Columbus Day in 1942.

Italian Americans were proud of Christopher Columbus, an Italian explorer, who came to the **Americas** hundreds of years earlier. Columbus Day became a holiday in New York in 1909. New York City held three parades that year.

Italian Americans in Tontitown, Arkansas, were famous for growing grapes. They even held a festival every year after all the grapes were picked. Today, the Grape Festival is more than 100 years old. Tontitown is named after Enrico Tonti, an Italian explorer.

Italian Foods

Food was a big part of every festival and holiday. For Christmas, Italian Americans made cannoli, a pastry filled with cheese, honey, sugar, chocolate, or fruit, and *zeppole,* fried pieces of dough sprinkled with sugar. Another special Christmas treat was *torrone,* nougat candy with nuts.

Italian Americans started many restaurants in the United States. The Cafe Bella Napoli in New York City's Little Italy is shown here in 1944.

24

Antipasto means "before the pasta." It was the first thing served at a meal. The Italian **immigrants** *pictured here in about 1910 probably enjoyed it at this meal in California.*

Family and friends got together on Sundays to enjoy a big meal. All kinds of foods were served. There was antipasto, a platter of cheese, olives, fish, salami, meats, fruits, and vegetables. There were meat and fish dishes and pasta dishes like lasagna and rigatoni. People from southern Italy were known for their pasta dishes. For dessert, there was *zabaglione,* a custard made with wine.

Many Italian Americans had gardens in their backyards. They would grow vegetables to use in their own cooking.

25

Music and Theater

Music halls and theaters were popular spots in cities. Italian Americans saw plays, **vaudeville,** and singers who performed **folk** songs and opera. Some theaters also had puppet shows. A popular Italian singer and actor in the United States was Farfariello. His real name was Eduardo Migliaccio. Large crowds came to see him perform. Audiences laughed at his skits about being Italian and living in the U.S.

Eduardo Migliaccio, also known as Farfariello, allowed Italians to laugh at themselves and the problems they had in life.

Later in his life, Arturo Toscanini conducted the NBC Symphony Orchestra. He is shown here in 1944.

Italian Americans loved listening to opera records. Later, they listened to opera on the radio. Opera was also performed at big concert halls in cities. At New York City's Metropolitan Opera, Arturo Toscanini, an Italian American, conducted, or led, the orchestra from 1908 to 1915. Enrico Caruso, a famous Italian opera singer, performed there many times.

I learned how to play the piano. My brother Fred became a violinist. With 25 cents a lesson, we used to go to . . . a little school, a music school.
—Charles J. Crimi, who came to the United States from Italy in 1911 when he was three

Louis Longo in the United States

Louis Longo worked hard in the United States. For many years, he worked at a company in New Jersey that made airplane parts. He also opened a pizzeria and restaurant in New York City. Louis cooked, and everyone in his family worked there, including Theresa, his wife. Louis loved living in the United States, but he never forgot where he was from and who he was, an Italian American.

Louis and Theresa outside their home in New York in 1946. In his spare time, Louis loved spending time in his garden.

Like many other Italian Americans, Louis spent a lot of time in Italy. He visited the rest of his family who lived there. And like many Italian Americans, Louis tried to help the country of Italy and the people who lived there. When he was older, Louis and Theresa visited southern Italy for months and helped take care of a church and its **orphanage.**

Today, Louis and Theresa's children live in the states of New York and New Jersey.

Louis, shown here with Theresa and their children, spent time with his family whenever he could.

When I was young, my grandfather gave me a ring that had been in our family for many years. He told me to pass the ring along to my son when I was older. Family was very important to my grandfather.
—grandson of Louis Longo, who is also named Louis

Italian Immigration Chart

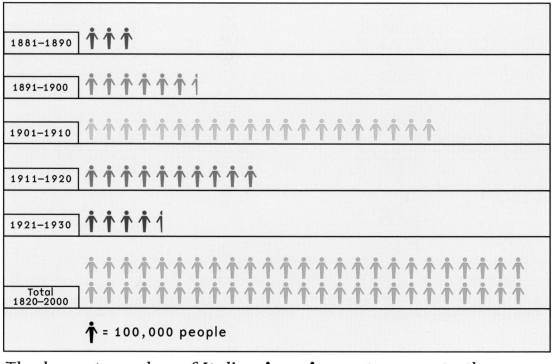

1881–1890	🧍🧍🧍
1891–1900	🧍🧍🧍🧍🧍🧍🧍
1901–1910	🧍🧍🧍🧍🧍🧍🧍🧍🧍🧍🧍🧍🧍🧍🧍🧍🧍🧍🧍🧍🧍
1911–1920	🧍🧍🧍🧍🧍🧍🧍🧍🧍
1921–1930	🧍🧍🧍🧍
Total 1820–2000	🧍🧍

🧍 = 100,000 people

*The largest number of Italian **immigrants** came to the United States from 1901 to 1910.*

Source: U.S. Immigration and Naturalization Service

More Books to Read

Bowen, Richard. *The Italian Americans.* Broomall, Pa.: Mason Crest Publishers, 2002.

Fahey, Kathleen. *We Came to North America: The Italians.* New York: Crabtree Publishing, 2000.

Petrini, Catherine M. *The Italian-Americans (Immigrants in America).* San Diego: Lucent Books, 2001.

Todd, Anne M. *Italian Immigrants, 1880-1920.* Mankato, Minn.: Blue Earth Books, 2001.

Glossary

altar table or stand used for religious purposes

Americas another name for North America, South America, and Central America

cholera disease of the intestines that people get from eating bad food or water

deck one of the open floors of a ship, which reaches from one side to the other

earthquake strong, shaking movement of the ground

ferry boat that carries people or things across water

folk having to do with the common people of a certain place. Folk music is the music played and written by the common people of an area.

godparent man or a woman who promises to make sure a child gets a religious education

harbor body of water where ships can drop their anchors

immigrate to come to a country to live there for a long time. A person who immigrates is an immigrant.

inspection examination

jewelry rings, bracelets, and other things made with jewels

malaria disease spread by an infected mosquito

nationality belonging to a certain nation

orphan child whose parents are dead. Sometimes, orphans live in places called orphanages.

peninsula land that is almost completely surrounded by water

port city near water where ships dock and leave from

priest spiritual leader of Roman Catholic religion

relative member of a family

Roman Catholic religion led by the pope that follows the teachings of the Bible

saint holy person

skyscraper tall building

steamship ship powered by steam

steerage place on a ship where passengers who pay the least to travel stay

tailor person who makes or fixes clothes

tenement house old, crowded apartment building in a poor section of a city

vaudeville show with a variety of different acts

Virgin Mary mother of Jesus Christ

Index